The Nifty Number 9

A Birthday Number Book

by Kitty Higgins

Illustrated by Peter Georgeson

**Andrews McMeel
Publishing**

Kansas City

www.andrewsmcmeel.com

The Nifty Number 9 is produced by becker&mayer!, Ltd.

ISBN: 0-8362-3215-1
Library of Congress Catalog Card Number: 97-70457

Edited by Alison Herschberg
Illustrated by Peter Georgeson
Book design by Simon Sung
Cover design by Heidi Baughman
Cover illustrated by Cary Pillo

Congratulations!
Happy birthday!
You are NINE years old!
You should feel lucky, because
NINE is a *nifty* number.
And this book will show you why.
Here we go!

Do cats have nine lives?

Actually cats don't have nine lives, they are just very clever and quick, managing to stay out of danger (and out of the way of barking dogs).

They also have the most wonderful talent of always landing on their feet! When cats fall, they can twist and turn their bodies so that their paws are the first things to hit the ground. Sometimes we say people who are very lucky "always land on their feet." Cats are great, but imagine if cats *did* have nine lives—there would be cats everywhere we went, and very few mice!

September is the ninth month.

September is usually the month that kids head back to school after a fun summer. But going back to school isn't that bad, because it also means that you are going back

to see old friends who you haven't seen for a long time. It means you get to tell everyone all the great things you did over the summer, like visiting neat places and meeting new friends.

September is also the beginning of autumn, football season, and cooler days—when you get to wear those new sweaters that you got for school. The ninth month, September, is a whole new beginning.

Are you on cloud nine?

Have you ever had one of those days when everything goes right? When everything that you say or do comes out perfectly? Doesn't it feel good? Sometimes we just feel so good it makes us feel like we're floating on a cloud. That is when people might say, "You look like you are floating on cloud nine!" I don't know why they call it cloud nine—it could have something to do with being nine years old, and having all the new responsibilities and adventures that go along with being older. But I do know that floating on a cloud is a great way to spend your day!

Pluto is the ninth planet from the Sun.

PLUTO

Pluto is a small, dark, frozen planet that's over 40 times farther away from the Sun than Earth is. It takes Earth one year to circle around the Sun, but it takes the planet Pluto 248 years!

A young American astronomer named
Clyde Tombaugh discovered Pluto in 1930
at the Lowell Observatory in Flagstaff,
Arizona. The dark planet was named after
the god of the dead in Roman mythology.
Charon (KEHR-uhn), Pluto's one known
moon, wasn't discovered until 1978.

The game of *croquet* has nine wickets.

Have you ever played croquet? If you have, then you know that the game is played on a lawn where wire hoops, called *wickets*, are stuck in the grass. Each player has a wooden mallet and a big wooden ball. The objective of the game is to whack the ball with the mallet and send it rolling through the hoops, which is not as easy as it sounds. There are nine hoops that you must get the ball through, and the other players are trying to keep you from getting your ball through the wickets by knocking it out of the way. The next time someone asks you to play, why don't you suggest croquet?

What noodle has nine letters?

There are foods that you eat with a fork, foods that you eat with a spoon, and some foods that you have to cut with a knife. There are even foods that you can eat with your fingers!

However, there is one nine-letter word for a long skinny noodle that is covered with a rich tomato sauce and sometimes big plump meatballs, and nobody can quite figure out how to eat it. Some people use a spoon, some people use a fork, and I'll bet there are some who have tried a knife—but I don't think *anyone* uses their fingers. Those slippery noodles spend more time sliding off your fork than they do in your mouth. Do you know what it is? SPAGHETTI!

Golfing a round with nine.

Did you know that golf courses are divided into two parts? There are eighteen holes in a golf course, nine at the front and nine at the back. There is also a golf club that is called a *nine iron*. It is used to hit the ball high in the air for a short distance. A nine iron would come in handy if you had to hit the ball over a big tree, or over the top of a house. Some golfers use the nine iron a lot! If you are nine years old and like to play golf, you could play the front nine with your nine iron. Now, *that* would keep the number nine busy for a while!

You can play Solitaire with nine cards.

Ever have one of those days when no one is home and there is nothing to do? How about playing a game of Nine Card Solitaire? You have to be very patient to play this game, and that's why in the old days it was called Patience.

A deck of cards can be a lot of fun even if you are not playing a card game. You can try standing them on edge and building a house of cards. Or if you are really in the mood to have fun, you can play Fifty-Two Card Pick-Up! You throw the deck of cards into the air and then pick them up!

Nine can help save the earth.

Now that you are nine years old, there are some very important things that you can do to keep the earth healthy.

Here are nine things that you can do to help:

1) Turn the water off while you are brushing your teeth.
2) Remind your family to recycle all aluminum cans.
3) Recycle the newspaper.
4) Recycle all those old tests you've taken—*all* paper can be recycled!

5) Add potato peels and other vegetable peels to a compost pile.
6) Walk or ride your bike, rather than asking for a ride in the car.
7) Donate your used toys and clothes to someone who can use them.
8) Bring your own canvas bag to the store instead of using a paper or plastic one (or if it is something that you can carry, don't use a bag at all).

...and last but not least,

9) Recycle the idea of recycling to your friends!

There are nine innings in a baseball game.

People play baseball all over the world. The game is played on a big field with two teams of nine players. And each game is divided into nine innings! What would the game of baseball be without the number nine?

In Major League Baseball, there are nine players per team. When they're out on the field, the players take the following nine positions: pitcher, catcher, first baseman, second baseman, shortstop, third baseman, left fielder, center fielder, and right fielder.

Some batteries have nine volts.

When it comes to batteries there are many different kinds. There are big batteries that help to charge up a car or boat engine, there are medium-sized batteries that are used to charge a lawnmower or a go-cart, and then there are the small batteries—the AA's, AAA's, C's, and the nine-volt battery. These are the batteries that put the flash in your flashlight, the rap in your radio, the roar in your roadster, and the fun in your toys. Batteries are great and so are nine-year-olds, but *you* don't come with batteries included!

Nine candles for Chanukah.

In December there is a Jewish celebration called The Festival of Lights, or *Chanukah* (HAN-uh-kah). Eight candles are placed in a candelabrum, called a *Menorah* (men-OH-rah) with eight

branches, and there is a ninth candle called the *shammash* (sha-MASH), which is used to light the other candles. On the first night a candle is lit, and each child in the family receives one gift. On the second night two candles are lit, and each child receives another gift. And on it goes for eight days! Doesn't that sound like fun?

The number nine plays ball.

When it comes to volleyball, the number nine is a very important number. On a volleyball court, the *service area*, the place where a player stands when she serves the ball, is nine feet nine inches square!

Volleyball is a fun game because all of the positions rotate. This means that each player gets a chance to play from every angle of the court. And when you're playing at the beach, the sand makes volleyball even more fun. Another spike for the number nine!

Now you are nine years old!

If you traveled to different parts of the world today, people might say "Happy birthday!" to you, and ask you how old you are. Here's how people might say this in Spanish, French, and German, and how you would answer.

Happy birthday! How old are you?
I am nine years old.

¡Feliz cumpleaños! Cuántos años tienes?
Tengo nueve años.

Bonne anniversaire! Quel âge as-tu?
J'ai neuf ans.

Glücklicher Geburtstag! Wie alt bist du?
Ich bin neun Jahre alt.

**Without a tail it is nothing.
What is it?**

The number nine.